THE AUTHORS
& PUBLISHER
OF HOWTOONS
HAVE MADE
EVERY
REASONABLE
EFFORT TO
ENSURE
THAT THE
PROJECTS &
ACTIVITIES
CONTAINED
IN THIS BOOK
ARE SAFE WHEN
CONDUCTED
AS INSTRUCTED,
BUT ASSUME NO
RESPONSIBILITY
FOR ANY INJURIES
SUFFERED OR
DAMAGES OR
LOSSES INCURRED
AS A RESULT OF
FOLLOWING THE INSTRUCTIONS
CONTAINED IN THIS BOOK.

PLEASE NOTE:
THE AUTHORS & PUBLISHER RECOMMEND
ADULT SUPERVISION
ON ALL PROJECTS!

ON A WONDERFUL LITTLE PLANET...

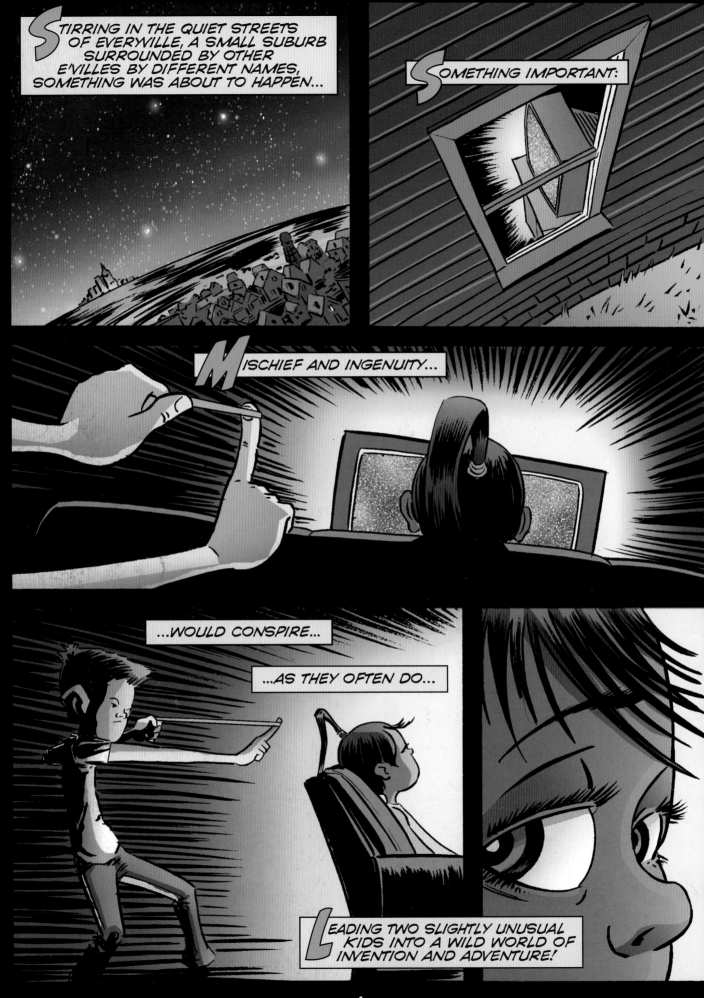

CHUCK JONES

HUBBLE

WINSOR McKAY RUTHERFORD LEONARDO DA VINCI ROALD DAHL ARCHIMEDES ORVILLE & WILBUR WRIGHT GOLDBERG

PAULING BABBAGE TERESHKOVA RUDE GIBBS

MENDELEEV JOSEPH BANKS RAMANUJAN JACK KIRBY TEZUKA ALEX TOTH BOHR

B. SHAKESPEARE STAN LEE FULLER WATSON & CRICK MARY SHELLEY JANE GOODALL PASCAL

BLODGETT ARTHUR GANSON H.G. WELLS COPERNICUS GAUSS FRANKLIN

FULLER BILL WATTERSON ERNEST SHACKLETON BELL DARWIN IFFE MAXWELL ADA BYRON LOVELACE CHRIS

LAVOISIER WILL EISNER HEISENBERG VON NEUMANN

CAPTAIN COOK FARADAY GUTENBERG BESSEMER LEE

MONTESSORI

HOWTOONS

THE POSSIBILITIES ARE ENDLESS!

Collins

An Imprint of HarperCollinsPublishers

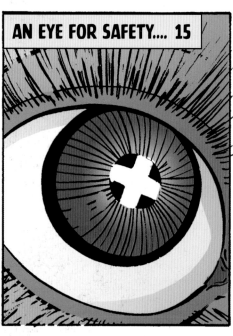

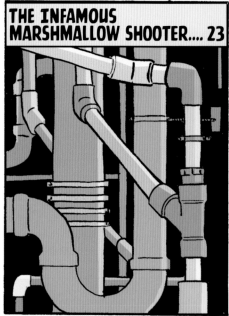
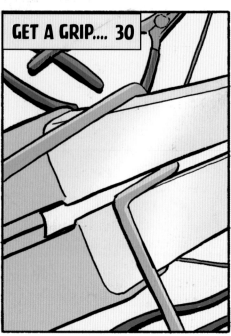
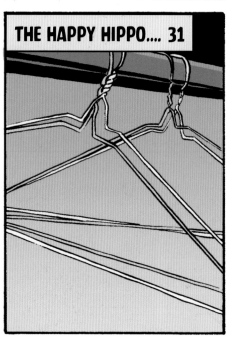

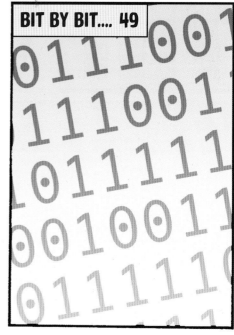

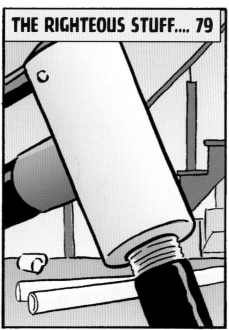

HOW, *adverb.*
A manner or method of doing something.
"The how of research is generated by the why of the world."

TOON, *noun. informal.*
A drawing depicting a situation, often accompanied by a word balloon or caption.

THE WORKSHOP

EVERY KID NEEDS A SPACE.

Hmmm. Where do we start?

Says here we'll need a workshop.

VIRGINIA WOOLF DESCRIBED IT AS "A ROOM OF ONE'S OWN."

HOW TO MAKE THINGS OTHER THAN TROUBLE

IT DOESN'T HAVE TO BE A ROOM, IT COULD BE HALF A ROOM, OR A CORNER, OR EVEN JUST A CUPBOARD, OR A SINGLE SHELF.

What do you think about THIS place?

THE IMPORTANT THING IS THAT IT'S A PLACE FOR YOUR BOOKS, DRAWINGS, TOOLS, TREASURES AND PROJECTS.

With a little clean up...it's perfect!

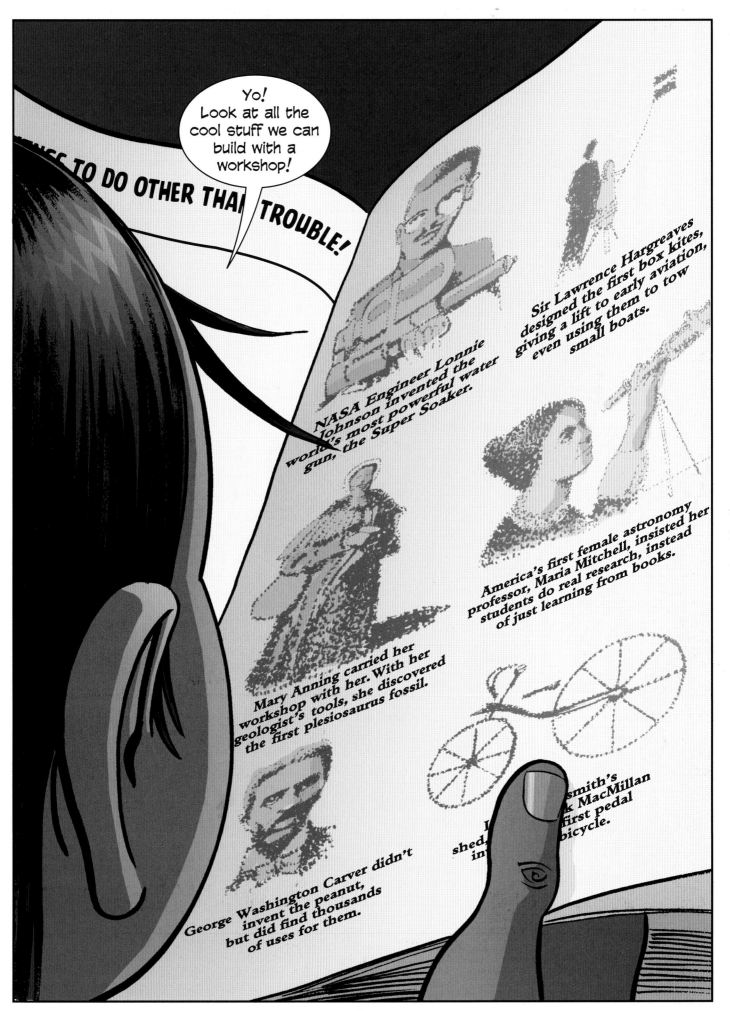

A MUSEUM OF YOUR MOST FANTASTIC FAILURES AND TREMENDOUS TRIUMPHS!

ORGANIZE YOUR SPACE! MAKE YOUR MAKING EASY, SAFE, FUN AND PRODUCTIVE. ALWAYS BE PREPARED FOR THAT NEW PROJECT.

BUT...DON'T LET IT GET TOO CLEAN — YOU'LL WANT TO FEEL FREE TO MAKE A MESS. OOH, AND HOW YOU WILL WANT TO MAKE SOME TERRIBLE MESSES.

ANATOMY OF A TOOL BUCKET

A STURDY PLASTIC BUCKET IS LIKE A PORTABLE WORKSHOP. ONE WITH A STRONG WIRE HANDLE IS GOOD. YOU CAN WRAP THINGS AROUND THE HANDLE TO MAKE IT EASIER TO CARRY.

HAMMER, SCREWDRIVERS, RULER, PLIERS, CUTTERS, SCISSORS, WRENCHES, CLAMPS, FILES, PENCILS AND BRUSHES, ADD A DRILL AND YOU ARE READY TO REPAIR, CREATE AND INVENT!

YOU CAN BEND HOOKS FROM COATHANGERS TO HANG USEFUL ITEMS LIKE ROPE AND CORD FROM THE SIDE OF YOUR BUCKET.

ALWAYS KEEP A ROLL OF DUCT TAPE AND A ROLL OF WIRE HANDY.

KEEP YOUR TOOLS SHARP, OIL THE JOINTS AND BEARINGS AND WIPE THEM CLEAN. DON'T DISCARD OLD TOOLS, THEY ARE OFTEN THE BEST, AND BROKEN TOOLS CAN BE USEFUL TOO. SOMETIMES YOU CAN CONVERT A BROKEN TOOL INTO A NEW TOOL FOR AN UNUSUAL JOB. IT HELPS TO WRITE YOUR NAME OR INITIALS ON YOUR TOOLS SO YOU CAN SHARE THEM WITHOUT CONFUSION.

ORGANIZE YOUR BUCKET TO EASILY LAY YOUR HANDS ON YOUR TOOLS. LIKE AN OLD WESTERN GUN-SLINGER, YOU SHOULD BE READY TO PULL THE PERFECT TOOL FOR THE JOB AT THE RIGHT MOMENT AS A MERE REFLEX. OLD JARS OR THE BOTTOM HALF OF SODA BOTTLES CAN BE USED TO SORT THE TOOLS INSIDE THE BUCKET.

A LONG TIME AGO, IN AN ERA OF EMPERORS AND KINGS...

TWO TRADERS TREKKED HOMEWARD AFTER A VERY SUCCESSFUL TRIP...

I hope the *king* is pleased with our *bonanza* of goods.

How could he *not* be delighted?

THE TRAVELERS' *MULE* WAS PACKED WITH *GOODS* FROM THE FOUR CORNERS OF THE *GLOBE.*

FROM THE *WEST AFRICAN* TRADING CITY OF TIMBUKTU THEY PURCHASED *SALT* MINED IN MALI AND SHIPPED ACROSS THE DESERT BY CAMEL — AT THE TIME SALT WAS WORTH ITS WEIGHT IN GOLD!

FROM THE *GLACIERS* OF NORWAY THEY CUT THE PUREST BLOCKS OF ICE, A *DELICACY* IN WARMER CLIMATES — THEY HAD TO MOVE *QUICKLY* WITH THEIR PRECIOUS QUARRY...

THEY FOUND *SUGAR* IN PERSIA, A VALUABLE COMMODITY THAT HAD MADE ITS WAY FROM *NEW GUINEA* VIA *INDIA* AND *CHINA*...

SUGAR

FROM *SPANISH* CONQUISTADORS THEY RECEIVED SOME OF THE FIRST SAMPLES OF THE VERSATILE *VANILLA BEAN* THAT WAS BEING CULTIVATED IN *MEXICO*.

IN NORTHERN EUROPE THEY FOUND THE *FRESHEST MILK* AND DIVINED THE *SECRETS* OF MAKING THE *THICKEST* CREAM!

A CLAY URN OF **SALT** CRACKED INTO THE HESSIAN SACK'S OF **ICE**.

THE POTS OF SUGAR, VANILLA BEAN, CREAM, MILK AND SPICES ALL BROKE INTO ANOTHER SADDLE BAG.

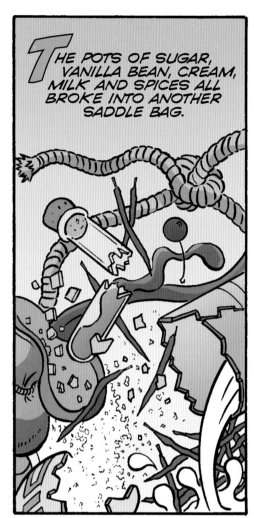

AND BY DIVINE FATE THAT **SADDLE BAG** FELL UPON THE OPEN SACK OF **SALT AND ICE!**

THE TWO GREAT EXPLORERS SAW THEIR INGREDIENTS **FREEZE** QUICKLY IN THE SALT AND ICE MIX.

Hey! All of the goods mixed up and made that giant mound of ice and cream.

With a *cherry* on top!

MANY OF THE WORLD'S GREATEST CREATIONS WERE BROUGHT ABOUT BY THE CAREFUL AND ENLIGHTENED OBSERVATION OF AN *ACCIDENT!*

Mmmm. Creamy-ice. *Smooth* and *delicious!*

The king *will* be pleased.

Provided you don't eat it all.

11

12

So that's *it?* *That* was the discovery of *ice cream?*
Yup, and it's taken scientists hundreds of years to *figure* out how it works.
HEAVY CREAM
BAG 1 ICE CREAM INGREDIENTS
1 CUP OF HEAVY CREAM
1/2 CUP OF WHOLE MILK
1/3 CUP OF SUGAR
3/4 TEASPOON OF VANILLA ESSENCE
The *secret* is in the thermodynamics! — How quickly we freeze the ingredients.
FLAVOR WITH CHOCOLATE CHIPS, NUTS, ETC..
BAGS ZIP
After mixing the components thoroughly, we pour them in our *first* bag.
It's *important* to squeeze all the *air* out.
Why?
Because still air is an *insulator* and heat doesn't pass *through* it.
That's why we use *double-pane* windows to keep the heat in.
COLD
STILL AIR
HOT
To *freeze* our ice cream the fastest, we don't want anything *insulating* our *ingredients.*

NOBODY KNOWS THE EXACT ORIGINS OF WHAT WE KNOW TODAY AS ICE CREAM. IN FACT, MANY CULTURES DEVELOPED SIMILAR ICE-BASED DESSERTS: SORBET, SHERBET, KULFI, GELATI, SNO-CONES AND ICE CREAM.

ALL THAT IS REALLY KNOWN IS THAT IT TOOK MANY ADVENTURES TO SCOUR THE WORLD FOR THE INGREDIENTS...

...AND A FEW EXPERIMENTALIST CHEFS TO CONVERT THEM INTO DOLLOPS OF DELIGHT!

Hey... uh... Celine! Do you want to take another ice cream break?

The End!

An Eye for Safety

THE BEST DEFENSE IS A GOOD IMAGINATION!

16

Last night I was running with scissors!

That one never ends well.

The night before that, it was jumping an unsecured bike ramp!

The list reads like an emergency room clipboard.

You're telling me.

Last night I cracked my thumb a mighty blow with a distracted hammer.

Later in the very same dream, I was climbing a tree, reaching for a branch...

...when my bandaged thumb lost its grip!

And gravity, as you know, is relentless.

I think Freud was right. My subconscious is trying to tell me something.

Freud? What do you mean?

It's my brain telling me to be more prepared, to foresee and avoid the danger.

Yeah, I guess our eyes and fingers are quite useful and worth protecting.

Maybe if we're more safety-conscious, our subconscious will stop giving us nightmares.

Hmm...

...you just reminded me that it will be vital to have safety glasses when operating my latest project.

Let's make safety goggles the first thing we do today.

I'll do anything to stop the nightmares!

We need a really tough piece of plastic.

The walls of an old soda bottle should do nicely.

CUTTING A SODA BOTTLE CAN BE TOUGH. SO START YOUR CUT BY STEPPING ON THE MIDDLE OF THE BOTTLE TO FLATTEN IT!

Cut the top and the bottom off the soda bottle, then cut the tube down the middle.

WARNING!

THESE GOGGLES ARE FOR BASIC PROTECTION, AND ARE NOT TO BE SUBSTITUTED FOR CERTIFIED SAFETY GLASSES WHEN THEY ARE RECOMMENDED.

Now place the soda bottle sheet on your face and trace the outline that you will cut.

The ear pieces and nose bridge are most important.

Feel free to design it any way you want.

Then, cut it out!

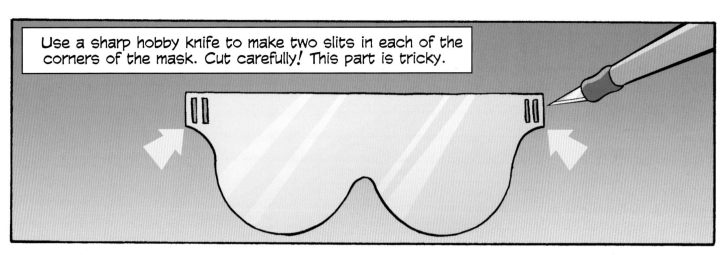

Use a sharp hobby knife to make two slits in each of the corners of the mask. Cut carefully! This part is tricky.

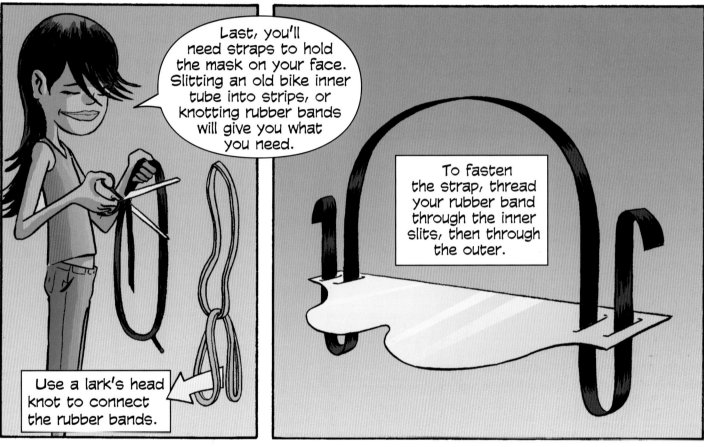

Last, you'll need straps to hold the mask on your face. Slitting an old bike inner tube into strips, or knotting rubber bands will give you what you need.

Use a lark's head knot to connect the rubber bands.

To fasten the strap, thread your rubber band through the inner slits, then through the outer.

Adjust and wear!

AHHHH!

I decorated mine with markers!

And I thought the NIGHTMARES were bad!

Grrrr.

The End!

CUT TO THE POINT

DOVETAIL SAWS
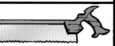
Clean, sturdy cuts, great for frames, cabinets and toys.

BACK SAWS
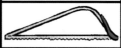
Thick-bladed with reinforced back for precision cuts.

BOW SAWS
Steel frame and blade for rough-cuts of wood.

CROSSCUT SAWS

For cutting against the grain. Can be used for many purposes from logging to detailed carpentry.

CROSS CUT TEETH Crosscut teeth are small teeth used to sever wood when cutting across the grain.

RIP SAWS
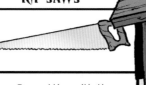
For cutting with the grain. The ripping action of the saw produces a coarse, ragged cut, which makes the saw unsatisfactory for finish work.

RIP TEETH Rip teeth are medium-sized teeth designed to scoop out wood fibers when cutting with the grain.

COMPASS SAWS

Small blade used for cutting curved or straight holes.

KEYHOLE SAWS

Intricate, close, inside work for specialty jobs.

COPING SAWS

Cuts irregular shapes and intricate patterns.

CUTTING

LINE OF ACTION

This is the correct cutting position. Your vision should always be true to the cutting plane, and always keep a straight line of action!

If possible use a clamp or vise to hold your piece and stop vibration.

1"
4 T.P.I.

T.P.I. stands for teeth per inch!
Rule of thumb: the more T.P.I. the harder the material the saw can cut!

THE HACKSAW

MOST VERSATILE OF ALL SAWS

CUTS PLASTIC / METAL / WOOD

UPKEEP A light coating of oil will make blades last longer. Be careful not to bend your saws. Hanging them up is a good method for storage.

30°

CUTTING ANGLES?

USE A MITER BOX!

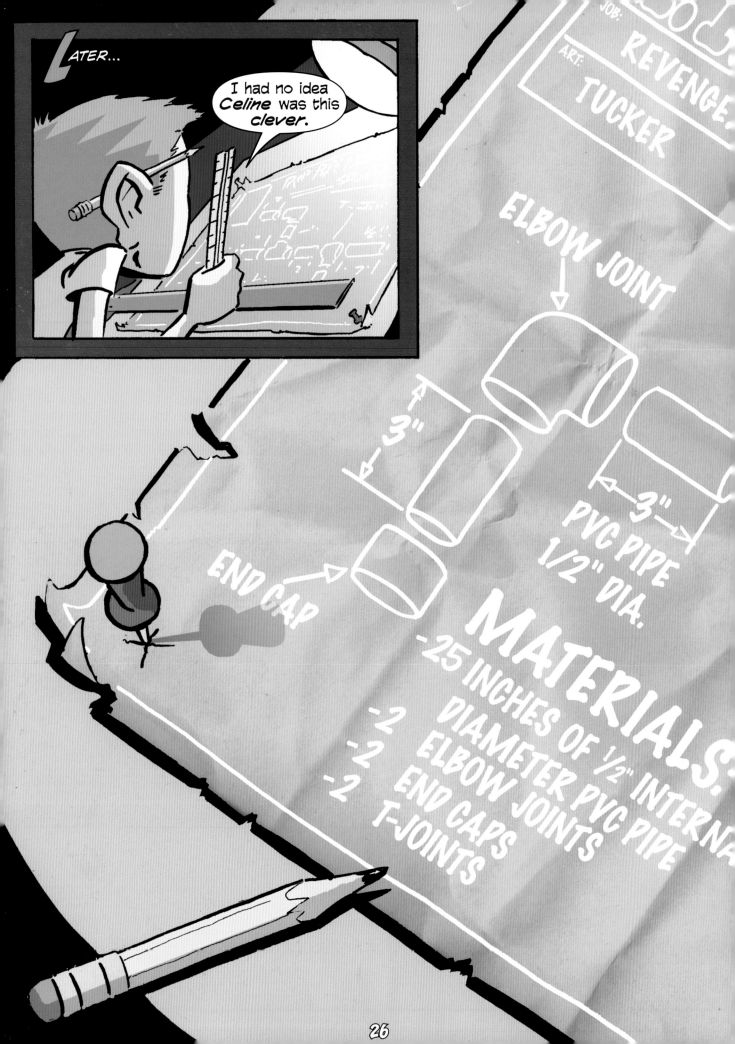

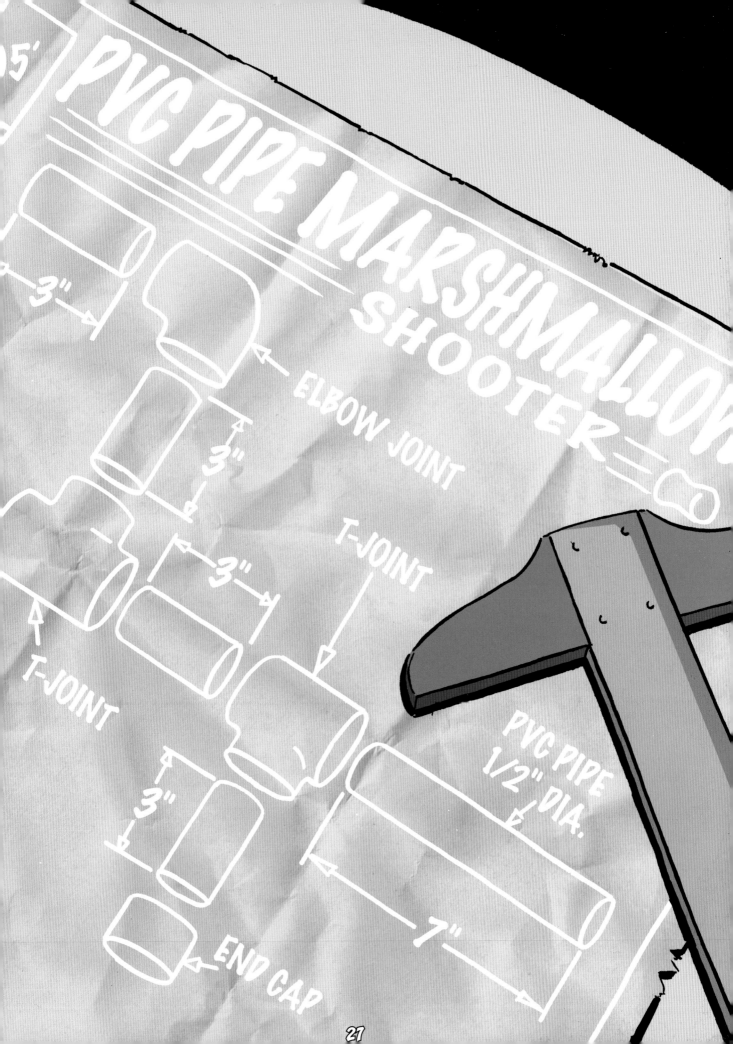

05' PVC PIPE MARSHMALLOW SHOOTER

3"

ELBOW JOINT

3"

T-JOINT

3"

T-JOINT

PVC PIPE 1/2" DIA.

3"

7"

END CAP

Load one *mini-marshmallow* at a time into the *mouth-piece.*

Seal your lips against the mouthpiece to avoid *air leaks*... and *loss of* POWER!

Blow as much *air* as possible in a *short, sharp blast.*

The *harder* you blow, the *farther* it'll go!

Always use *fresh mini-marshmallows.*

When the marshmallows are *soft,* they create a better *seal* against *air leaks.*

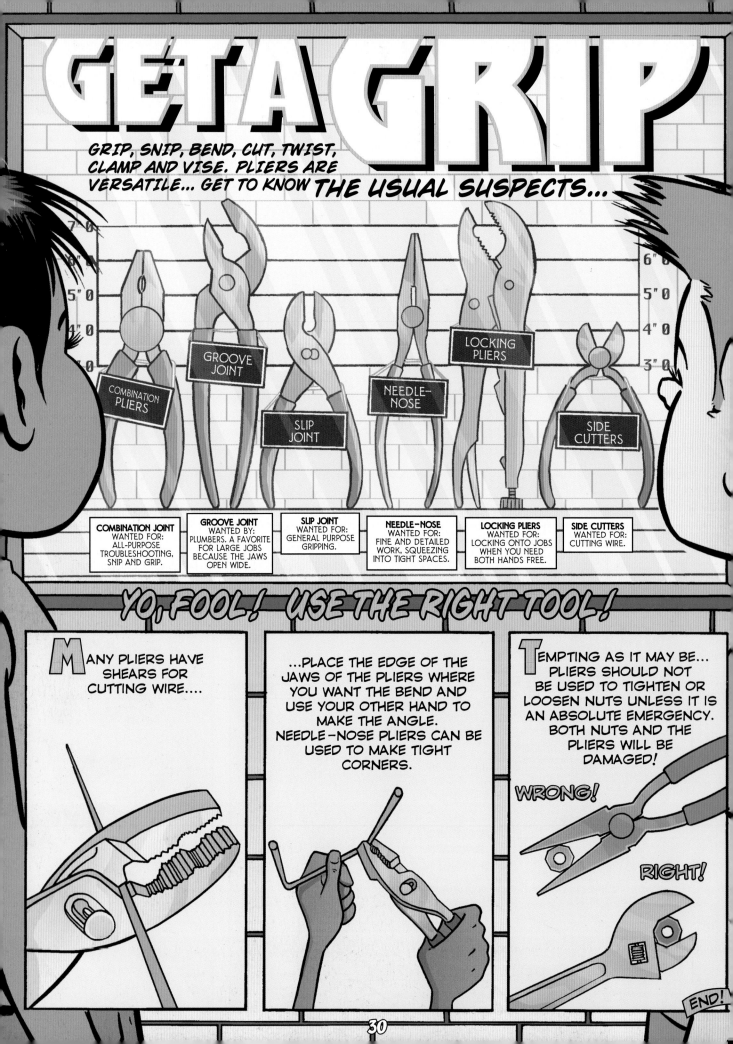

GET A GRIP

GRIP, SNIP, BEND, CUT, TWIST, CLAMP AND VISE. PLIERS ARE VERSATILE... GET TO KNOW **THE USUAL SUSPECTS...**

COMBINATION PLIERS

GROOVE JOINT

SLIP JOINT

NEEDLE-NOSE

LOCKING PLIERS

SIDE CUTTERS

COMBINATION JOINT
WANTED FOR: ALL-PURPOSE TROUBLESHOOTING, SNIP AND GRIP.

GROOVE JOINT
WANTED BY: PLUMBERS. A FAVORITE FOR LARGE JOBS BECAUSE THE JAWS OPEN WIDE.

SLIP JOINT
WANTED FOR: GENERAL PURPOSE GRIPPING.

NEEDLE-NOSE
WANTED FOR: FINE AND DETAILED WORK, SQUEEZING INTO TIGHT SPACES.

LOCKING PLIERS
WANTED FOR: LOCKING ONTO JOBS WHEN YOU NEED BOTH HANDS FREE.

SIDE CUTTERS
WANTED FOR: CUTTING WIRE.

YO, FOOL! USE THE RIGHT TOOL!

MANY PLIERS HAVE SHEARS FOR CUTTING WIRE....

...PLACE THE EDGE OF THE JAWS OF THE PLIERS WHERE YOU WANT THE BEND AND USE YOUR OTHER HAND TO MAKE THE ANGLE. NEEDLE-NOSE PLIERS CAN BE USED TO MAKE TIGHT CORNERS.

TEMPTING AS IT MAY BE... PLIERS SHOULD NOT BE USED TO TIGHTEN OR LOOSEN NUTS UNLESS IT IS AN ABSOLUTE EMERGENCY. BOTH NUTS AND THE PLIERS WILL BE DAMAGED!

WRONG!

RIGHT!

END!

The Happy Hippo

THE LION MAY BE KING OF THE JUNGLE, BUT SURELY THE HIPPO IS LORD OF THE LOWER LEVELS.

ITS NATURAL ENVIRONMENT IS A LUXURIOUS, AROMATIC SWAMP.

AMIDST TREES, FOLIAGE, FELLOW ANIMALS AND DENIZENS OF THE DEEP, THE HIPPO LURKS, STALKING GRASS IN PRODIGIOUS QUANTITIES.

They're beautiful.

INDEED, THE HIPPO IS NEVER HAPPIER THAN WHEN IT SHARES ITS INNER ESSENCE WITH THE WORLD.

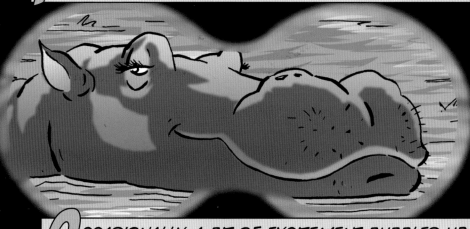

OCCASIONALLY, A BIT OF EXCITEMENT BUBBLES UP.

I will capture the inner essence of the hippo if it's the last thing I do!

The *wire* coat *hanger*, for example, is one of the most *versatile raw materials* in existence.

And a simple *pair* of *pliers* is all I will *need* to *bend* it to my *will*.

First I'll cut the length!

That should do.

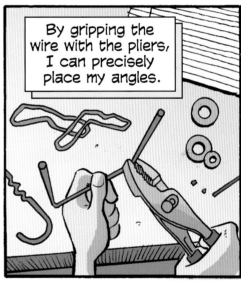

By gripping the wire with the pliers, I can precisely place my angles.

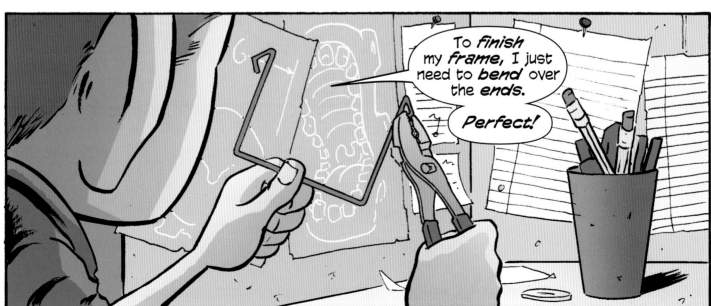

To *finish* my *frame*, I just need to *bend* over the *ends*.

Perfect!

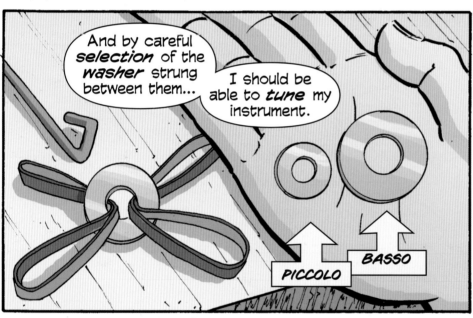

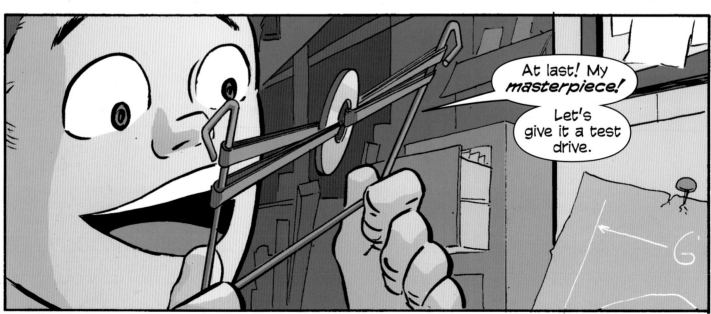

35

The BEST THINGS in LIFE are FREE

See, Celine, I told you that garbage Santa existed... look at all this awesome stuff he has left us!

The important thing is to see the world for what it could be, not for what it is. Coat hangers, soda bottles, inner tubes, rubber bands, cardboard, wood and plastic... and this cool jar! We've got everything we need!

You know, Celine, it might be even better if we collect these things before they hit the trash heap. That'll save us from diving around in this stinking Dumpster.

TERRARIUM

A terra-
what?!

A terrarium,
Tucker.

Hmm...a
terror-arium!

No, Tuck, a
terrarium. It's one of
many different types
of vivarium.

It's a
container, usually
glass, and sometimes
sealed, for observing
flora and fauna.

A paludarium is
a miniature rainforest,
a riparium is a mini river...
Terrariums are generally
simulating dry climate
areas...

Formicariums
are ant farms, and
insectariums are
for insects.

A NICE BIG PICKLE JAR WITH A LID WILL WORK NICELY. YOU COULD USE A FISH TANK, OR EVEN A LARGE SODA BOTTLE WITH THE TOP CUT OFF.

P LACE A FEW INCHES OF DIRT IN THE JAR, WITH PEBBLES ON THE BOTTOM TO GIVE IT BETTER DRAINAGE.

F ILL THE TERRARIUM WITH EVERYDAY THINGS YOU FIND IN NATURE: ROCKS, STICKS, WORMS AND INSECTS. IF YOU BUILD A REALLY LARGE ONE, YOU CAN TRY SMALL LIZARDS.

S MALL SHADE AND WATER-LOVING PLANTS ARE BEST, LIKE CLOVER OR SMALL FERNS. MOSSES AND LICHEN WORK VERY WELL, TOO!

B UT BEWARE! CREATURES NEED TO EAT! IF YOUR TERRARIUM CAN'T SUPPLY ENOUGH NUTRIENTS, YOU WILL HAVE TO FEED THEM.

P LACE THE JAR WHERE IT WILL RECEIVE PARTIAL SUNLIGHT. WATER ONCE IN THE BEGINNING, BUT NOT TOO MUCH, OR THE PLANTS WILL ROT. THE WATER VAPOR WILL STAY IN THE JAR AND BE CONTINUALLY RECYCLED.

Y OU CAN LEAVE THE TERRARIUM OPEN AT THE TOP BY PUTTING SMALL HOLES IN THE LID. THIS WAY IT CAN GET NUTRIENTS FROM THE OUTSIDE WORLD AND SURVIVE A LONG TIME. IF YOU SEAL IT COMPLETELY, YOU ARE RUNNING AN EXPERIMENT IN CLOSED ECOSYSTEMS. THE NUTRIENTS FROM THE SOIL FEED THE PLANTS, AND THE NUTRIENTS FROM THE PLANTS FEED THE INSECTS, AND THE CARBON DIOXIDE NEEDED BY ALL LIVING THINGS WILL HAVE TO BE BALANCED PERFECTLY BY THE WHOLE SYSTEM.

IT'S TIME TO...
PUMP IT UP!

NO STEROIDS. NO PROTEIN POWDERS. NONE OF THOSE TEDIOUS HOURS AT THE GYM... FOLLOW OUR STEP-BY-STEP GUIDE TO INSTANT MUSCLES.

First, put the old T-shirt on the old person.

Ha... old!

Next, taking strips of the duct tape, fully cover the T-shirt. Two layers will do.

Using the scissors, carefully cut up the back of the shirt and duct tape.

Easy, sis.

Now just wriggle the old person out!

Then we tape up the seam in the back where we cut.

Well, Tuck... Try it on!

Wow!! This is really gonna bulk me up!

The End!

48

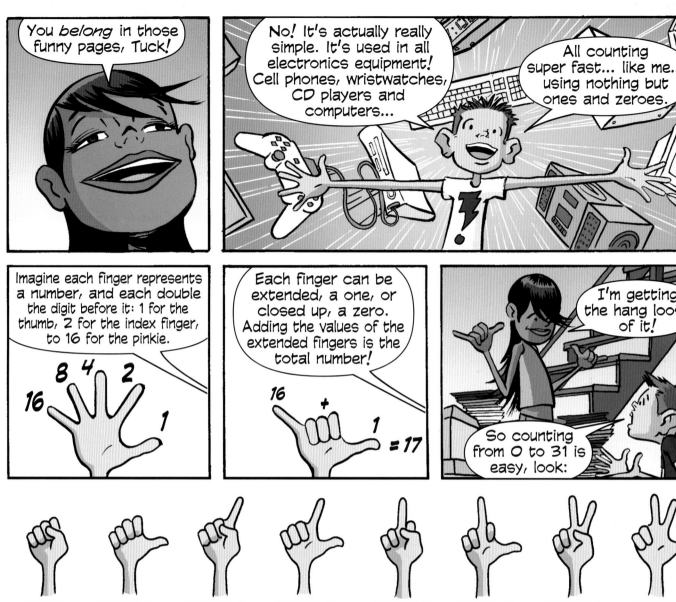

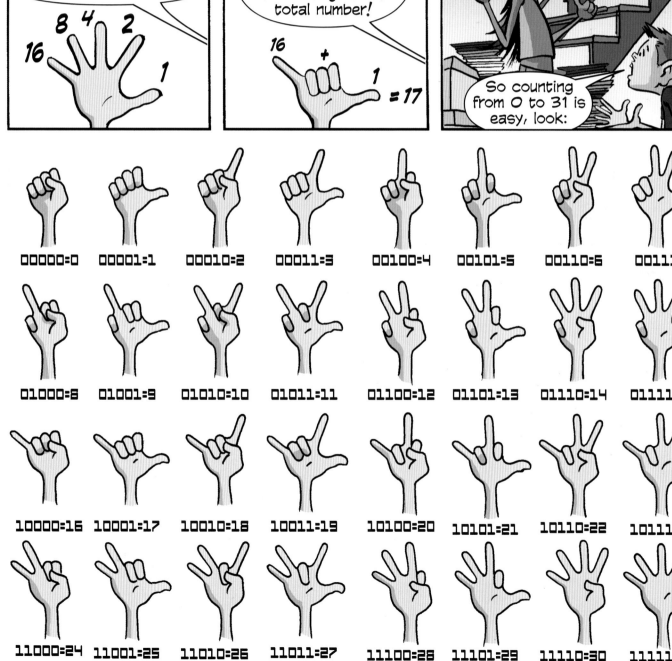

Then to get to 1023, I simply add my next 5 fingers ... 32, 64, 128, 256, 512.

I can even go over a million when I use my toes. 1,048,575 to be precise ...

That stinks, Tuck.

No not at all, this binary counting system is what makes everything work.

Robots...

...computers...

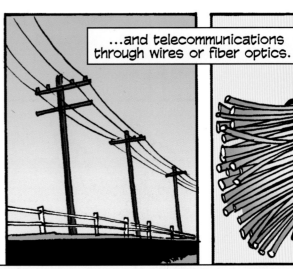

...and telecommunications through wires or fiber optics.

In electronics, the zeros and ones are represented by high and low voltages, or flashes of lights, not by my fingers... A zero or a one is called a bit.

It's all a bit hard to believe, Tuck! Get it? Bit hard ...!

Only if you byte off more than you can chew!

The End!

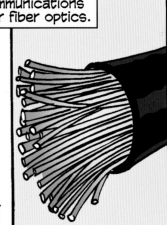

110100

Legend of the Monkey Fist Clan

*Always employ an experienced adult in the choice of a tree and installation of a tree swing.

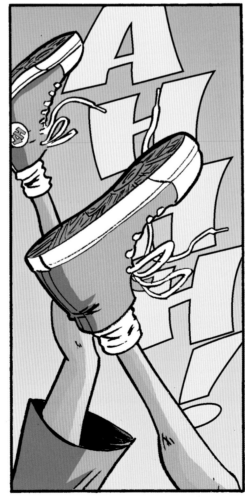

A shipwrecked family of seafaring arborists, the Monkey Fist Clan had to survive on a deserted island with nothing but their knot-tying tricks and rope skills to aid them.

In order to survive they learned to use rope for everything; their braids, knots, splices and weaves transformed the desolate environment into a treehouse paradise.

To throw their ropes, the clan developed a heaving knot, the Monkey's Fist. Mastery of this decorative, yet functional, knot was the first sign of adulthood.

Start with a light line, 1/4 – 1/2" in diameter.

Holding one end between the forefinger and the thumb, wrap the first three coils around your hand, then slip those loops off.

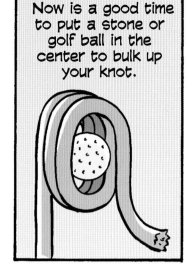
Now is a good time to put a stone or golf ball in the center to bulk up your knot.

You are ready to coil in the opposite direction.

Like so... be careful to keep the first three loops open.

Now you are ready to put the final three loops back through the first three.

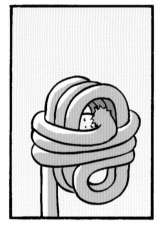

You're almost done!

You'll need to tidy the knot by carefully working backward, pulling the slack and pulling it tight as you go.

This knot takes some patience and learning...

...but has many decorative uses as well as utility in throwing.

Voilà! Our heaving line is ready for action!

Pick a branch with a fork. This is what keeps your line from sliding down the branch.

When choosing your branch make sure it is sturdy and has live foilage at the tips. If it is still alive it will be strong, not rotten!

Heave the monkey fist over that branch, Tuck!

Sweet toss!

The next important knot is the sheet bend. It's the oldest known knot, dating back 9,000 years.

The sheet bend will join the lightweight heaving line,...

...which is the tail end of your monkey's fist...

...to the sturdy piece of rope we'll use for swinging from the tree.

Use at least a 5/8" line for tying around the branch.

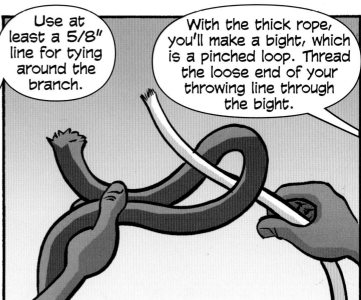

With the thick rope, you'll make a bight, which is a pinched loop. Thread the loose end of your throwing line through the bight.

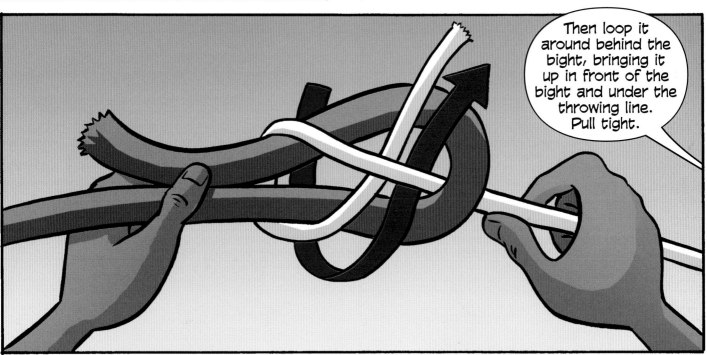

Then loop it around behind the bight, bringing it up in front of the bight and under the throwing line. Pull tight.

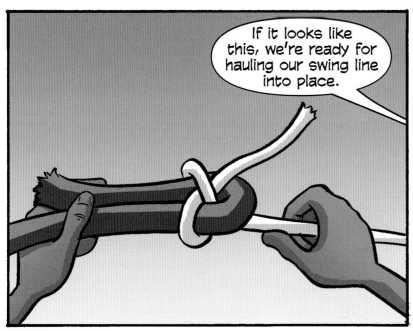

If it looks like this, we're ready for hauling our swing line into place.

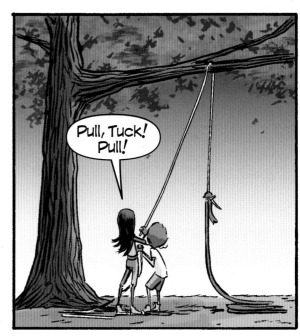

Pull, Tuck! Pull!

We tossed the rope through the fork so we can tie the swing at the base of the tree with a killick hitch.

This means we'll be able to remove the rope easily when we are done and reuse it for future trees.

We no longer need the heaving line, so we can untie the sheet bend.

I was wondering about that.

Watch closely.

How are we going to tie up our loose ends, sis?

We need something to sit on...

And this branch should do nicely.

The final knot we need is...

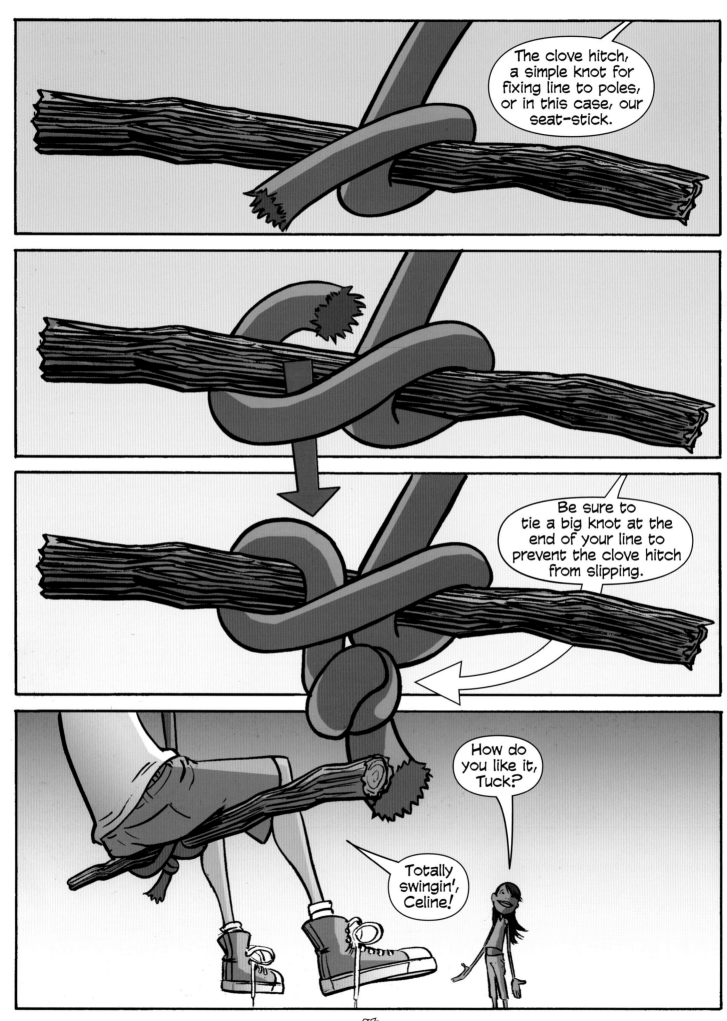

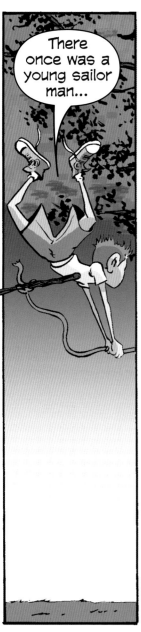

There once was a young sailor man...

Who grew up with the Monkey Fist Clan.

A half hitch on the bight...

And knot tying foresight...

Let him swing through the sky as he'd planned!

There was a strange boy named Tucker... For limericks he was such a sucker...

The End!

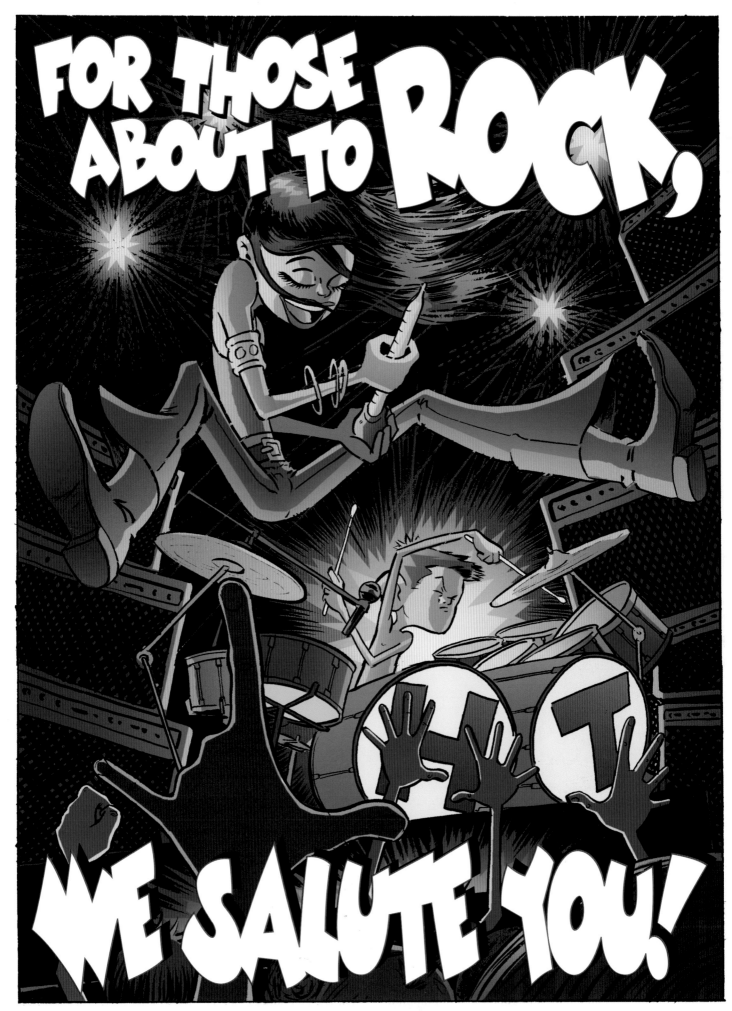

Swinging, huh?!

I'm thinking of starting a band!

Can I join the band?

Can I join the band?

Can I join the band?

Can I join the band?

Pleeeeease... Pleeeeeease...

Look, sis... I think it's cool you want to be in the band.

I really do.

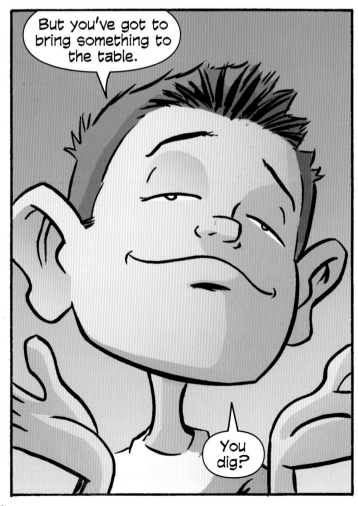

But you've got to bring something to the table.

You dig?

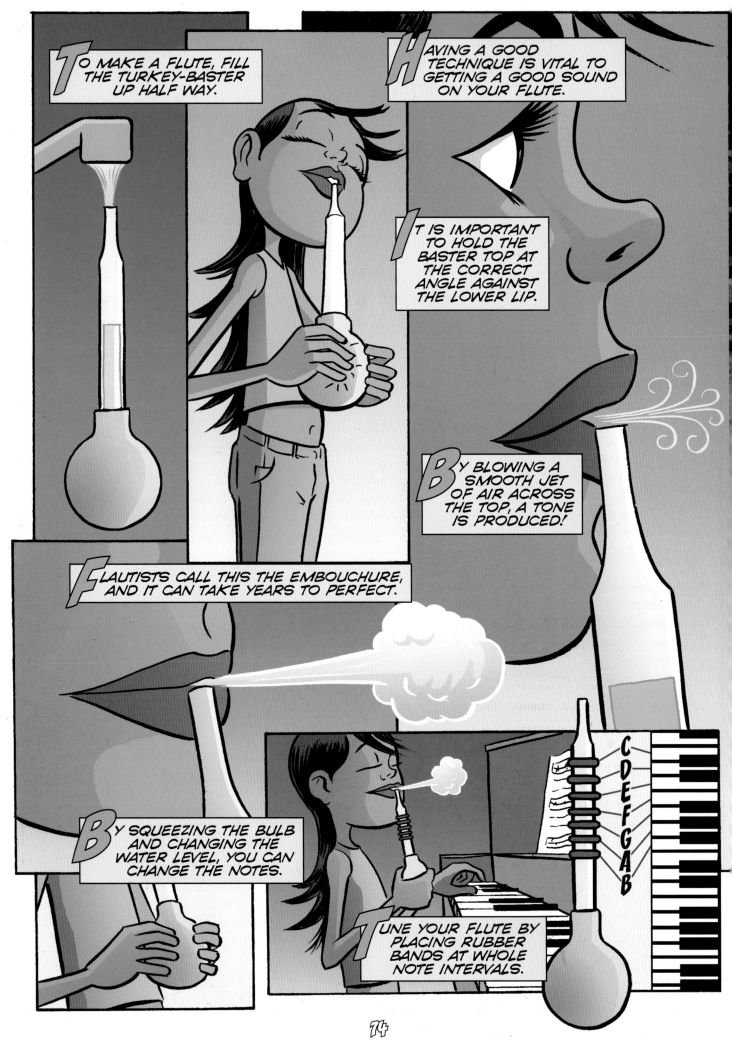

Building your own super-simple electric motor is easy, given a little patience and some simple objects.

The key to making the electric motors that drive everything from forklifts to toothbrushes is the coil of insulated wire. As a current passes around the coil it turns the loop into an electromagnet. The permanent magnet and electromagnet then push and pull on each other to create motion.

The safety pins conduct electricity up from the battery into the coil.

You'll need some insulated wire. 22 gauge magnet wire is ideal because it comes with an enamel (insulating) coating.

The ends of the coil act as an axle.

The safety pins act as the simplest possible "commutator"; that's what makes everything work. As the axle rotates in the safety pin, it turns the current from the battery on and off each rotation, which turns the electromagnet on and off.

A permanent magnet provides the driving force by repelling the magnetic field induced in the coil.

C- or D-cell battery.

A rubber band will hold your safety pins to the battery, and the magnet will stick to the battery naturally.

Neodymnium rare earth magnets are the strongest and will really make this motor fly.

Start with your magnet wire.

Wrap it 10-12 times around a C- or D-cell battery.

Wrap the loose ends 3-4 times around the coil you have created and cut a 2-3 inch axle on both sides.

To make your motor really spin you will need to balance its coil. It needs to be symmetrical about the axle.

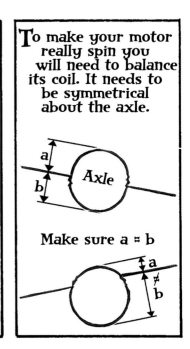

Make sure a ≈ b

To get the electricity into your coil, you need to remove the insulation from the wire at both ends of the axle.

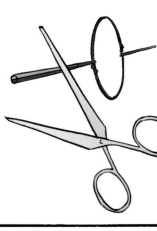

A knife or one blade of a pair of scissors will do this perfectly.

Carefully scratch the insulation off one side of the axle.

Threading the axle through the safety pins and connecting them to the battery allows the current to pass through.

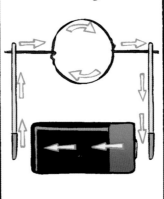

The current in the loop induces a magnetic field. The rubber band holds everything in place.

The induced magnetic field is north poled on one side of the coil and south poled on the other.

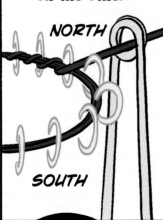

NORTH

SOUTH

This field is repelled by the permanent magnet and kicks the coil over.

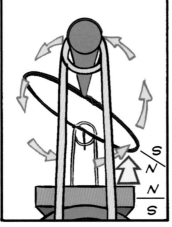

When the insulated side touches the safety pin, the field turns off and the coil can spin right around to do it all over again.

As it spins, the motor gets a little magnetic kick on every revolution, keeping it spinning.

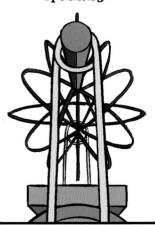

THE RIGHTEOUS STUFF

GO WHERE NO KID HAS GONE BEFORE

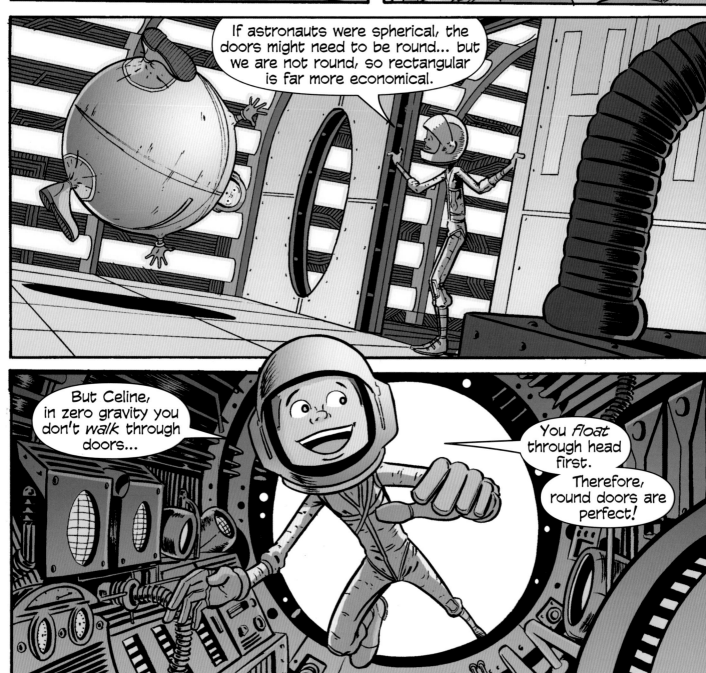

Sometimes the ship will land on a planet with gravity. Then how are you going to float through your round doors?

We've agreed on safety protocol, soda bottle fuselage, and the air fuel source... but as you obviously cannot see the advantages of my round doors...

I've got no choice other than privatizing my space program.

Fine! Let the space race begin.

Hmmphhh!

That stubborn $%#*?!

At THE LAUNCH SITE.

I'll launch first.

Fine! Let's set 'em up.

Ready, Tuck?

My systems are go.

Me too!

Safety systems enabled.

And the energy source is ready...

Start pumpin', Tuck! Ready in 3...2...1...

Blasss....

NOOOOOOO!

My design was also flawed, Tuck. Looks like neither of us will go to space at this pace.

We were too gung ho. A space program isn't built in a day. Let's put differences aside and work together...

How about we sign an inter-neighborhood space treaty?

I'd be honored to work with you, Tuck!

Trying to launch a soda bottle really *is* rocket science.

We'll need to draw from everything we've ever built to pull this thing off!

Celine! That's it.

The modified marshmallow shooter.

What are you thinking?

It might not have worked for marshmallows...

...but it's got serious rocket-launching potential.

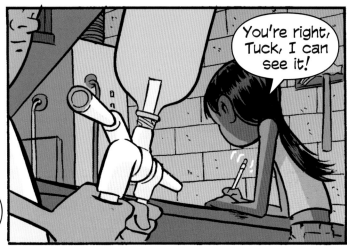

You're right, Tuck, I can see it!

Check this out... it might just work.

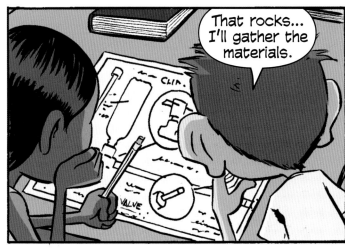

That rocks... I'll gather the materials.

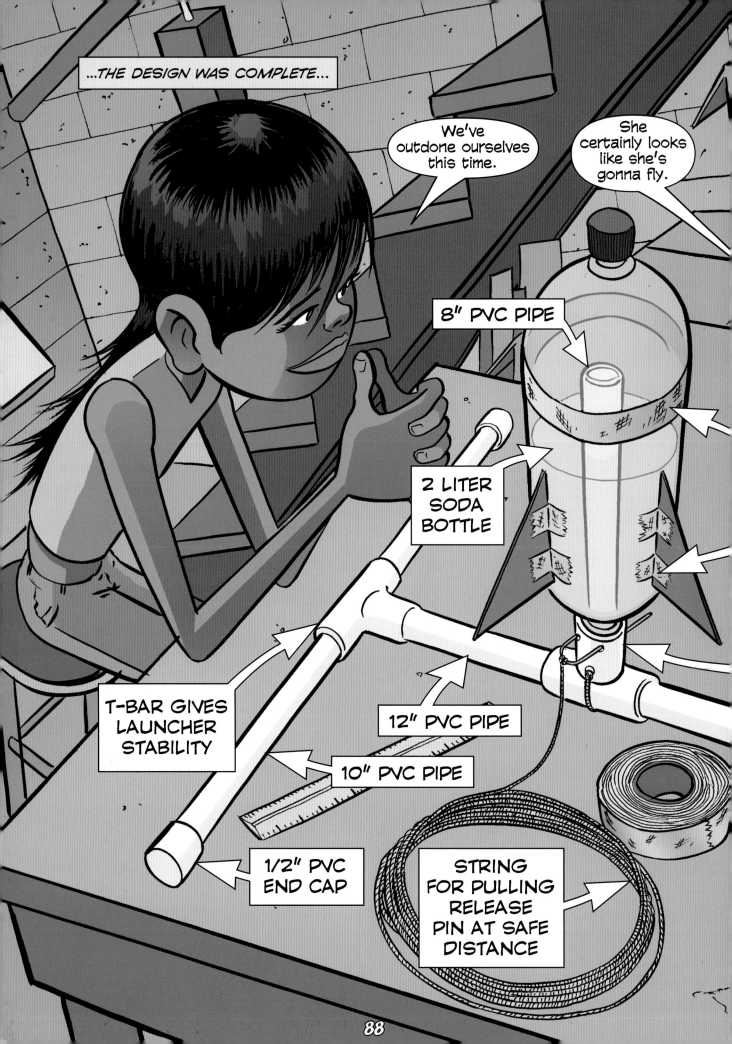

The air valve is one of the most important features. We need a great seal.

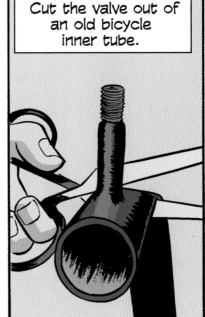

Cut the valve out of an old bicycle inner tube.

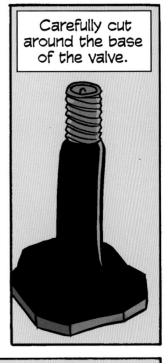

Carefully cut around the base of the valve.

Now we need to drill a hole in the 1/2" PVC end cap.

You'll want a 5/16" drill bit straight through the center.

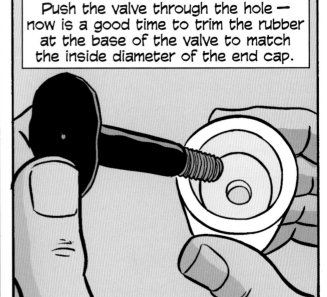

Push the valve through the hole — now is a good time to trim the rubber at the base of the valve to match the inside diameter of the end cap.

Finish it off by pulling the valve all the way through. It will be very tight — for a good seal — so you may need to grasp it with pliers.

90

Now for the most critical job of all — the O-ring rocket booster seal.

Mark the pipe at 1.25 inches.

Carefully file a groove all the way around the pipe. You may need to try this more than once.

The groove needs to be just a little shallower than the O-ring.

Slide the O-ring onto the pipe...

...and into the groove.

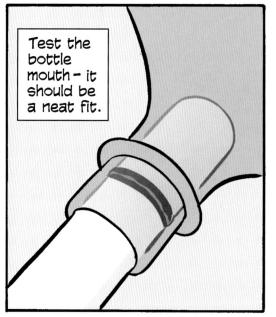

Test the bottle mouth - it should be a neat fit.

If not, file off the high points or start again.

Tip: a little soap on the O-ring will help glide the rocket into position.

Now that the
subcomponents are ready,
it is time for assembly.

You will need PVC glue,
which is toxic! So be sure to
apply the glue in a place with
good ventilation so you don't
breathe the fumes.

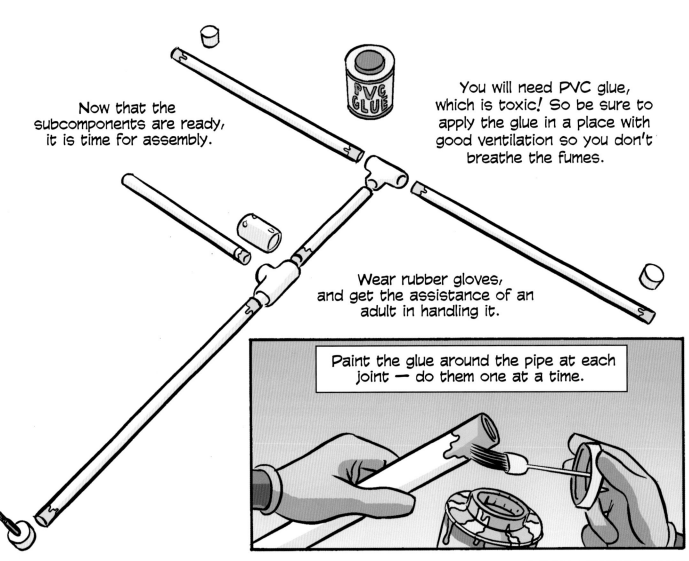

Wear rubber gloves,
and get the assistance of an
adult in handling it.

Paint the glue around the pipe at each
joint — do them one at a time.

Place the
valve assembly
on firmly.

Glue the remaining
T-joints and end caps.

The launch mechanism requires some monkey clan skills and some of the usual suspects...

A little wire-bending hippo technology too.

With the same 5/16" drill bit, drill two holes in one end of the 1" connector...

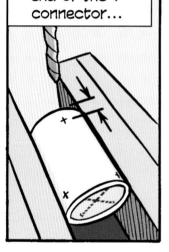

...and four holes in the other end.

Cut an 8" length of coat hanger and bend it halfway around a piece of 1/2" pipe.

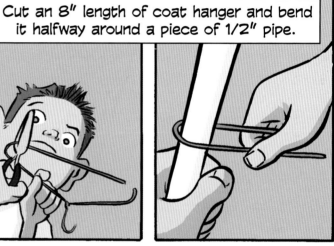

The coat hanger will sit through the four holes like this and grip the top lip of the bottle.

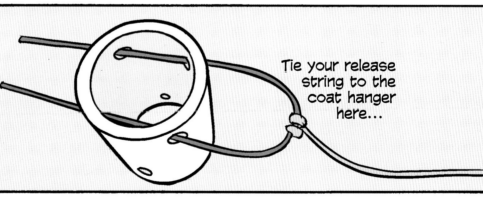

Tie your release string to the coat hanger here...

Finally, we need to attach this release mechanism to the main body of the launcher — Start by tying one end of a piece of string through one of the bottom holes.

Slide it onto the launch tube.

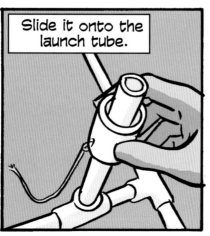

Wrap the string under and tie it through the hole on the other side.

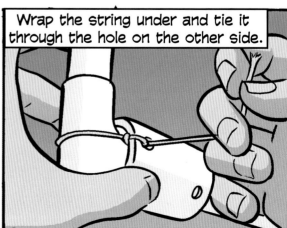

93

And of course the last thing you'll need is a rocket!

You can leave a message in your bottle for the aliens who will find it once it reaches orbit — or you can figure out a way to pack a parachute in there.

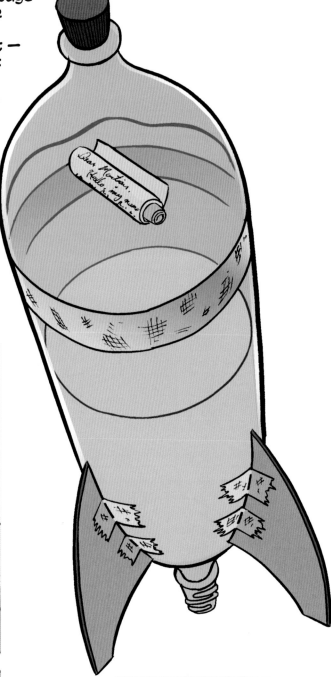

For the aerodynamic nose cone, cut the top off a second bottle...

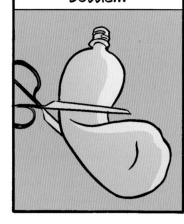

And tape it around the bottom of the main bottle.

And after all that work, we can finally fill the rocket with the power source — plain tap water will do.

For the fins, cut some fin shapes from cardboard...

...and tape them firmly to the outside of the bottle.

The stabilizing fins should be symmetrical and aligned with the flight direction!

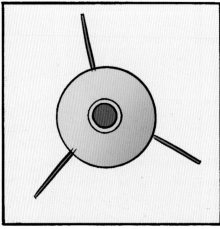

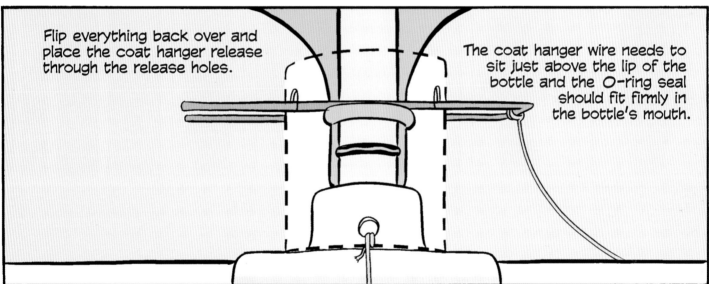

PING

GLOSSARY

AERODYNAMICS: This is the study of the way objects move through gases such as air. An object can be considered highly aerodynamic if it meets with little resistance, or "drag," as it moves through the air.

ARBORIST: Also known as a tree surgeon. They are lucky people who get to climb trees all day and care for them. Kind of like vets for plants.

ARMATURE: The rotating coil in electric motors and generators. In our motor, it's the 10 loops of copper wound around the battery.

BASSO: A deep, low singing voice.

BEND: A knot tying two lines (ropes) together.

BIGHT: When you bend a piece of rope to make a knot, it is called a bight. This U-shaped section of rope is useful in forming many knots. Threading the end of the rope around or through the bight is what creates the knot.

bight
loop
standing end
elbow
working end

BINARY: Describes a system that has two parts or modes (on or off, black or white, 1 or 0). Binary describes the base 2 counting system employed at the heart of modern computers.

BIT: This is the fundamental unit of computation as we know it. It is the name for the 1, or the 0, in binary digits.

BOOB TUBE: This is an antiquated, derogatory term that the artist's mother used to describe a television to those who watched it too much.

BRAID: Three or more things can be interwoven into a braid. Ropes and hair are often braided, but rarely together!

BYTE: 8 bits in a row are called a byte. 00100001 is a byte that represents 132.

CENTIMETER: 1/100th of a meter. It is a commonly used unit in metric measurement. There are 2.54 centimeters in one inch.

COMMUTATOR: The device that switches the direction of current in the armature of an electric motor so that it always goes one way.

CONDUCT: This term is used in science to describe movement through things. Heat conduction describes the movement of heat through a material. Electrical conduction is the movement of charge (or current) through a material.

CURRENT: In the same way that current describes the flow of water in a river, it describes the flow of charge in an electric circuit.

DRAINAGE: The process of draining the liquid from something. Allowing the water to flow to the bottom of your terrarium is drainage for the soil on top.

ECOSYSTEM: In ecology, an ecosystem describes all the living and non-living things in an area. The bacteria and dust in your navel (or belly button) might be described as its own ecosystem.

EMBOUCHURE: The shaping of the lips and movement of face muscles required to make wind instruments work.

FOOT: 12 inches long, or 12 X 2.54 = 30.48 centimeters. Very few people have feet that are a foot long.

FOSSIL RECORD:
In the layers of earth beneath us lie the amoeba plants and dinosaurs that used to live on Earth. The order of the layers tells us much about our origins. The fossil record resembles a layered cake of history, with the oldest layer on the bottom.

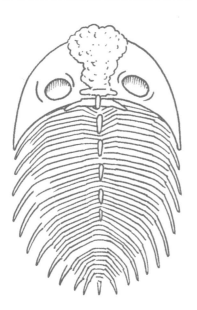

FREEZING POINT: This is the temperature at which a liquid, such as water, turns into a solid, such as ice.

FUSELAGE:
The body section of an airplane.

FUSELAGE

GAUGE: A tool for making measurements, like a pressure gauge, or a strain gauge, or a fuel or gas gauge.

GRAVITY: The force between two masses. The earth has a huge mass, which means it has a very strong force that pulls your small mass toward it. This has an unfortunate tendency to make you fall toward the ground.

HESSIAN SACK: Also known as burlap, hessian is a heavy woven fabric made principally from jute and other vegetable fibers.

HITCH: A hitch is any form of knot that ties off to a post or ring.

INCH: 1/12th of a foot.

INSULATOR: Thermal insulation slows the flow of heat, while electrical insulation slows the flow of electricity.

LIMERICK: A short and generally humorous poem with a strict format. It's typically five lines long, with an A-A-B-B-A rhyming pattern (this means that the first, second and last lines rhyme with each other, and that the third and fourth lines rhyme with each other).

MAGNET: Originally found in Magnesia in Ancient Greece, the word magnet came to describe materials where a magnetic polarity could be stored. The magnetic poles act upon each other to exert force, either attracting or repelling each other.

NORTH   SOUTH

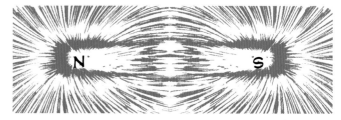

MASS: The mass of an object is kind of like the weight, except that it doesn't change if you move to planets with less gravity, whereas your weight does.

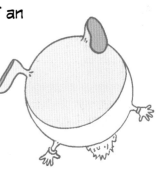

METER: The international standard unit of length. There are 100 centimeters in a meter.

MILLIMETER: 1/1000th of a meter. There are 25.4 mm in an inch. 10mm in 1cm.

NUTRIENTS: A nutrient is food for an organism. The marshmallow in your navel is a nutrient for the bacteria there.

NUTS: Nuts screw onto screws, or bolts. They are often hexagonally shaped donuts with a screw thread in the middle. Like donuts, the right one can be hard to find when you need it.

OCEANOGRAPHY: This is the study of the oceans and the seas of the world. It is becoming increasingly important in terms of understanding global warming and the heating of the oceans. More than 70% of the earth is covered in water; most of it is in the oceans.

PICCOLO: This is a fancy Italian word for a small flute, but can refer to any tiny musical instrument.

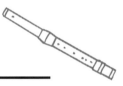

PLANE: Mathematically a plane is a two-dimensional surface, like a sheet of paper. A plain sheet of planar paper can be folded into a paper plane. A three-dimensional paper plane can fly.

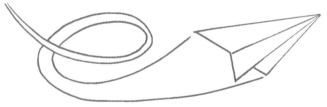

POLLUTE: A foreign or toxic item in an ecosystem is a pollutant. Pollution should be avoided. Things like soda bottles should be recycled or reused rather than tossed into the environment where they pollute.

PVC: Polyvinylchloride is the plastic material more commonly known as PVC. It is used a lot in construction, and sometimes in the construction of toys.

ROBOT: A robot is a machine that is programmed to do things. They eat, sleep, and dream in binary.

SAFETY PROTOCOL: A set of guidelines to help you do things safely.

SCOPE: This is the suffix for many technical instruments used to look at or observe something, such as microscopes and telescopes.

SHEARS: The general term for big scissor-type things. Because of their large handles with lots of leverage, they can cut thick things.

SIGN LANGUAGE: Combines hand shapes and positions into an entire language that is often used by deaf people.

SPLICE: If you braid the end of a piece of rope to the end of a piece of hair, it would be called splicing. Splicing joins two ropes end to end.

SYMMETRICAL: An object is symmetrical, or has symmetry, when it is a reflection through a plane or a rotation around an axis. Your face is mostly symmetrical around the plane of your nose. A soda bottle is symmetrical about the axis that runs from the center of the base to the center of the cap.

THERMODYNAMICS: This is the branch of physics that studies the movement of energy, often in the form of heat, in a system.

VOLTAGE: The measure of the electrical potential of something. The more volts, the more jolts.

WEAVING: Two sets of threads are woven together to create fabric; the process is called weaving. The

warp is the direction the weave comes out of the weaving loom, and the weft is the thread that passes along the length of the loom. You can remember that the weft goes west (if the warp goes north to south!).

WOOD GRAIN: The patterns in a piece of wood caused by the alignment or growth direction of the wood fibers.

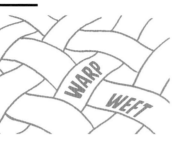

YARD: 3 feet or 36 inches long. A yard can also be a great place to play in, and should be many yards long.

Collins is an imprint of HarperCollins Publishers.

Howtoons: The Possibilities Are Endless
Copyright © 2007 by Howtoons LLC.
All rights reserved. Printed in the U.S.A.
No part of this book may be used or reproduced in any manner whatsoever
without written permission except in the case of brief quotations embodied in
critical articles and reviews. For information address HarperCollins
Children's Books, a division of HarperCollins Publishers,
1350 Avenue of the Americas, New York, NY 10019.
www.harpercollinschildrens.com

Library of Congress Catalog Card Number: 2007924969
ISBN 978-0-06-076158-5

Designed by Nick Dragotta and Comicraft
2 3 4 5 6 7 8 9 10
❖
First Edition